Why Donald Trump Should Not Be Pr

Bob Navarro

2022

Dedicated to my Angel, Espy

Foreword

After four years as President, Donald Trump was a disaster in almost everything that he touched. His only accomplishments were a tax cut, which mostly benefitted the corporations and rich people, and the building of a new partial fence between the United States and Mexico that only totaled 40 miles. In foreign affairs, he did manage to create Jewish relationships with a few Arab countries. Domestically, instead of focusing on infrastructure, Trump spent his time attacking Muslims, trying to overturn the ACA, removing environmental regulations, restricting immigration, and deporting thousands—and playing golf on his golf courses, which ended up being over 300 times.

He was impeached twice, investigated by the Mueller inquiry, and was sued repeatedly for his actions. He created fissures in our political system and in our mutual society. Instead of trying to unify the nation, Trump used his presidential pulpit to demonize perceived adversaries, especially the media, as well as members of his own administration. With his thousands of tweets, he lambasted a broad spectrum of issues, including the BLM movement and racial inequality. With his appointment powers he reshaped the judicial system, including the nomination of three right wing Associate Justices to the Supreme Court. He withdrew the United States from several multilateral agreements, invoked tariffs that only hurt American consumers—especially the farmers—tried to bring back manufacturing to the United States, attacked NATO, and downplayed the deadly coronavirus pandemic. He was singularly responsible for the emergence of misinformation as he aligned himself with questionable groups such as QAnon. And after he lost the 2020 election, Trump embarked on a quest to overturn the results of the Electoral votes, including inciting an insurrection to prevent the election certification of Joe Biden.

In the end, President Trump left the nation in disarray with an uncontained coronavirus pandemic, a near-depression economy, a spiraling national debt, an armed capital city due to an insurrection, a divisive population because of his hateful words, a failed vaccine distribution plan, a food insecurity crisis, an increased structural inequality, no infrastructure projects, the insolvency of one-fourth of the farming community due to his tariffs on China, a fractured relationship with our closest allies and NATO, a dismal failed foreign policy with regards to Russia, China, Syria, North Korea and Iran, and with no resolution to the wars in Iraq and Afghanistan. Why anyone would want Donald Trump as President again is a mystery, considering the devastation that he caused in his four years in office.

Contents

Introduction

When Donald Trump launched his presidential bid in 2015, he rode down an escalator in Trump Tower, using the media attention to promote his own brand and property. He lied, he made racist remarks about Mexicans being rapists and murderers, and he exaggerated the crowd size at the Trump Tower, for which he paid people to have them attend. In every way he showed what type of President he would become if elected. The rest of his campaign, including debates with 16 other Republican candidates, was no different. He continued to stoke racial tensions, to bully everyone that criticized him, and to demean anyone who crossed him. During the time that he was running for President, he was secretly involved in a proposed Trump Tower project in Moscow, Russia.

Republican leaders offered assurances that a Trump presidency would be different. They said that the burdens of the office would transform him and that he would have a competent team of aides, seasoned staffers and career Republicans who would provide the policy for his administration. Thus, they abdicated their responsibility and instead of putting the country first, they chose instead to elevate Trumpism in all its forms.

But Trump stayed exactly as he was during the campaign. He abandoned his populist promises to pursue the trickle-down policies of the past. He continued to make racist and sexist remarks, and to pursue policies that enabled him to use the presidency to enrich himself and his family. Instead of focusing on infrastructure and using the opportunity to rebuild the country, he opted to abuse his power. Even so, Republicans supported him in almost every way—including the appointment of Amy Barrett to replace Ruth Bader Ginsberg on the Supreme Court right before the 2020 election as well as his previous appointments of Neil Gorsuch and Brett Kavanaugh as Associate Justices to the Supreme Court.

He railed against Blacks, Asians, and Latinos as he promoted a white nationalist agenda by emboldening White Supremacists. He criticized the BLM movement, calling them terrorists. He looked upon President Andrew Jackson as a hero—someone who removed the Indian population of five tribes from the Eastern United States. He protected statues of Confederates and refused to have the names of military installations named after Confederates to be changed, citing the need to preserve heritage.

Trump lied about the size of his crowd at his inauguration—which was a lot smaller than the one for President Barack Obama—in his first full day in office, and the untruthful tone was set for the next four years. He tweeted over 26,000 times. He called the media "the enemy of the people" over 2,900 times. He lied about small and large matters, such as claiming that his tax cuts were the largest in American history. Trump's fraudulent pitch as a successful businessman was seen by most Americans as the failure who he always was—a con man instead of a businessman, the epitome of a P. T. Barnum character.

The Perennial Liar

Trump's whole presidency was filled with lies. The *Washington Post* kept track of his comments and counted 30,753 misleading claims during his four years in office, with one-half of them being said during his final year. Even after leaving office, he has continued to lie saying such things as "that he requested 10,000 National Guardsmen for his January 6th rally, but that Speaker Nancy Pelosi rejected it," and "Gas prices were $1.86 a gallon when I left the White House".

Trump is a successful liar because he refuses to remember. He also refuses to remember the current moment in the future. Thus, he lives mainly in the current moment such that future consequences don't matter to him. An example was when he had trouble going down a plank at a military ceremony on a sunny day. Later he recounted the same event saying that it was rainy, and his shoes were very slippery. Hence, his current lies will not matter to him. And since he has lived his entire life this way to great acclaim and success, then why would he ever want to change?

Trump never pulls back on blatantly false statements—lies that are so obvious that they defy logic and common sense. Instead, he immerses himself in an angry, combative moment, striving desperately to win the moment. Psychologists have stated that for Trump, it is as if he wakes up each morning nearly oblivious to what happened the day before. What he said yesterday no longer matters to him. And what he will say today will not matter for him tomorrow.

Truth for Trump is whatever works for him in the moment. He tells you exactly what he thinks in the moment. He lies straight to your face, without shame and without any concern for future consequences. Thus, Trump will tell a blatant lie–and insists on it, even in the face of clear evidence that it is a lie. That is who he is.

Trump is incapable of telling the truth because his whole life has been based on lies and deception. He does not listen and only likes to hear himself talk. He also does not understand because he is not aware of what is so. He merely translates events according to his conditioning—depending upon his mood, which is mostly dour. Moreover, he is indifferent to the chaos that he creates. In many ways he is confused since he wants to be right all the time—no matter what transpires. He is brutal and destructive with a lazy mind that is caught up in self-deception, and which only leads to isolation from everyone

His Lack of Empathy

Trump lacks the ability to understand and share the feelings of another. He does not care, nor does he have a desire to help others. None of his emotions can ever match another person's emotions, nor can he discern what another person is thinking or feeling. His past experiences, especially with his father, have had a very negative influence that prevents him from having empathy for another person.

Trump's lack of empathy surrounding the coronavirus pandemic was evident in how he handled it. People were scared yet he repeatedly and publicly downplayed the severity of the COVID-19 virus—including when he told Americans, "Don't be afraid of the virus" before leaving the military hospital where he was treated for the virus—which almost killed him—in October 2020. He even compared the virus to the flu despite its virulent and contagious deadliness. He showed little concern about the staggering number of Americans who died of the coronavirus; and was instead focused on how well the stock market was doing. Although in March 2020 he did advise the American public to stay home, for the most part he was against shutting anything down because the economy was more important to him than people getting sick and dying. Thus, he issued an executive order to keep meat plants open despite hundreds of meat workers coming down with the coronavirus.

The worst part is that he ridiculed the wearing of masks and offered quack cures for the coronavirus, He pushed drugs such as Remdesivir, Hydroxychloroquine, and Chloroquine, suggested using ultraviolet light to combat it, and even proposed injecting bleach as a method of killing the virus within the body.

His Lack of Awareness

Trump is not fully aware of the real issues in life. Otherwise, he would understand what is going on and he would not resort to condemning and criticizing others. He is insensitive to nature and people, and he functions from habitual patterns of behaviors that he has accumulated through time. He gets bored and loses interest in issues that are too complicated for him to digest and analyze. He thrives on sensationalism, exploitation, and false excitement in a process of creating problems where they sometimes do not exist. He narrows and limits the circumstances to influence events toward his views.

Trump uses hate as a barrier with words that are geared as an impediment to understanding. He creates disparaging nicknames for persons that he despises, he resents being questioned about his actions, and he becomes angry when events close in on him. He is mean, he never forgives people, he never apologizes for anything, and he sometimes uses gossip to put forth unsubstantiated claims. He is certainly not generous in his donations to society. He approaches matters by bragging that "he is richer and smarter" than anyone else.

His desire to interfere with others has no limits or boundaries. He is cruel and ugly, and he uses distractions to avoid dealing with issues and to offset criticisms. At best, he has a superficial interest in world events, and he obtains his information from television shows that are slanted toward his views. He fills his life with material things, and almost every weekend he escapes from everything by playing golf. In his conscious mind, he never pays attention to the deeper concerns in life, but rather focuses on insignificant and trivial matters. It is a limited and biased awareness of the world where every challenge is met with his innate prejudices—and with total arrogance.

Immigration Vilification

Trump turned out to be the worst version of what some people feared as President, especially regarding immigration. He obsessed with vilifying immigrants, with his first action being an executive order to ban Muslims from seven Muslim majority countries—none of which ever perpetrated any terrorism within the United States—from entering the United States. This left people stranded in airports, being unable to reunite with their families. An estimated 42,000 people were deprived of visas. While the initial ban was blocked by the courts, he cut refugee resettlement to record low levels. He went after sanctuary cities and raided Pentagon funds to pay for the construction of his medieval fence between the United States and Mexico. He was driven by a quest to deport as many undocumented immigrants as he could.

His most aggressive action was for immigrants detained at the border, including children. He instituted a zero-tolerance policy that separated more that 4,200 children from their parents at the border without having any plan to reunite them. Many of these children were permanently separated from their parents with whereabouts unknown. The Trump administration put children in temporary holding facilities, such as cages, with many of them being locked up for months. Many of these children remain apart, and over 1,000 of them contracted the coronavirus while in custody.

Trump shut down asylum and other legal relief in the courts and implemented the "Remain in Mexico" policy to force asylum seekers to wait in Mexico for court hearings. And once the coronavirus pandemic started, the Trump administration began to turn away people at the border entirely using the disease as the reason. He also used ICE to round up hundreds of illegal immigrants and deport them without any compassion whatsoever. ICE arrested over 144,000 illegal immigrants and made a total of over one million apprehensions.

Trump tried but failed in changing the birthright citizenship that is accorded to all babies who are born in the United States—regardless of their parent's status. He did end the diversity lottery, which grants visas to people from nations that he derided as "shithole countries". He also cut family reunification visas associated with chain migration. He had Attorney General Jeff Sessions officially end the DACA program by decree. Although he was blocked from ending the DACA program by the courts, his administration delayed renewals until a Supreme Court ruling overturned it. Nevertheless, he successfully ended the DAPA program, which affected 11 million illegal immigrants.

Trump wanted to exclude undocumented immigrants from the 2020 census so that they would not count for the new redistricting in 2021 but was blocked by the Supreme Court. He cut back on TPS extensions, H-1B and H-2B visas or immigrants, with the latter affecting over 10,000 health care professionals that were badly needed to deal with the coronavirus outbreak. Trump also denied immigrants from obtaining green cards and Visa applications that use public benefits such as Medicaid, food stamps or housing assistance.

Trump always depended on focusing the ire of his supporters at minorities. When Trump first hit the political scene in 2015, it was with a speech attacking immigrants, specifically Mexicans, in what would be a preview of his campaign and presidency. In the end, Trump spouted the same rhetoric about minorities, but in a slightly different way, baselessly claiming that Democrats, buoyed by voters of color, stole his election in the hopes of hijacking America. He insisted that millions of undocumented persons voted illegally, thus stealing the popular vote from him.

Trump also aimed to exclude noncitizens from the 2020 census. This was because he wanted to leave an older and whiter population counted in states with large immigrant populations, presumably to work towards Republican advantage during reapportionment. Bur he failed to reach his goal to eliminate the counting of undocumented immigrants as time ran out on his legal attempts.

The Petulant Child-Man

Trump acts like a petulant child and refuses to follow the rules. His decision to not wear a mask was deplorable, especially when the CDC was urging everyone to do so whenever social distancing was not possible. He portrayed the worst message possible, essentially saying "I don't care about you, I don't care about your health, I don't care about your welfare, and I don't care about anyone but myself". After he lost the 2020 election, he gave a nonsensical and paranoid tirade about how apparently if Trump loses the election, then it was all rigged against him, and if he wins, then everything is fine. He called President Biden ungracious after for not acknowledging the accomplishments of his administration during an address to a joint session of Congress.

He acts like a four-year-old because it's the thing he can't help but do and the thing he has always done. That is why Trump is always at his worst when he tries anything: to speak from a teleprompter, to feign compassion, to organize a sentence, to remain on message, or to take the high road. Nevertheless, Trump appears to be trying all the time, laboring restlessly, compulsively to be noticed, to win, to dominate the room, to avenge slights, to force reality into the shape of his fantasies, or just to read the world around him properly. The Trump dissonance is that he is an elderly man who possesses the outward appearance and trappings of adulthood—and who occupies the public role that we associate with adulthood—but who is on the inside, predominantly infantile.

Trump seeks happiness through gratification. In his mind he seeks a permanent state that he deems to be the truth. But he is incapable of knowing the truth because he is trapped in a world of illusion and delusion. He escapes into an antagonistic state of mind, and then does not understand the aftermath because he has no self-knowledge. It is an infantile approach that only leads to failure and frustration. All that he can do is blurt out opinions—which are not the truth--but only serve as propaganda. He is an unscrupulous man who is trying to be virtuous. Yet he continues to lie incessantly—and to pout like the spoiled brat that he has always been.

The Perversion of Justice

Trump devastated the standing of the DOJ and the FBI. He also used the DOJ to protect his political interests and to punish his enemies. He ignored restrictions to prevent contacts between the DOJ and the executive branch. He unleashed a campaign against the FBI, beginning by firing the FBI director, James Comey, on a false pretense—merely because Comey was investigating him. He accused the FBI of being behind a plot to take him down. He forced his Attorney General, Jeff Sessions to resign because Sessions recused himself from any involvement in the Russia probe of Trump's involvement with Russia's interference during the 2016 election. He got the next Attorney General, William Barr, to alter the findings of the Robert Mueller investigation to protect the President from being indicted—even though he also made him resign eventually when Barr stated that the 2020 election was fair and accurate. Before the 2020 election, he tried to get the DOJ to attack his political rival, Joe Biden, by going after his son, Hunter Biden. And he tried to get the DOJ to investigate what he viewed as a fraudulent election after he lost. Even after Barr left at the end of 2020, Trump tried to install Jeff Clark as Attorney General to have him declare the 2020 election as fraudulent and therefore null and void.

The Trump administration increased the pace of federal executions by executing 13 persons—including a woman, the first in 70 years. This made Trump as the most prolific execution President since 1896 and exceeded the total for all 50 states combined. Most of these were Blacks. When demonstrators started to protest the killing of Black men by the police, he sent Gestapo officers in hoods and masks without badges to quell the disturbances. He even wanted to send in troops to the cities where protests were occurring but was denied from doing so by the Secretary of Defense.

At the end of his presidency, he pardoned convicted felons: the notorious sheriff of Arizona, Joe Arpaio; the ex-Governor of Illinois, Rod Blagojevich; the financier, Michael Milken; a federal procurement official, David Safavian; his former national security advisor, General Michael Flynn, and his long-time ally, Roger Stone, who had intimate knowledge of Trump's doings. He finished his presidency by pardoning 100 persons, which included white collar criminals and a rapper.

He was able to nominate three Supreme Court Associate Justices: Neil Gorsuch, Brett Kavanaugh and Amy Barrett, with the last one being done with only 3 weeks before the 2020 election. He packed the District and Appeals Courts with almost 300 conservative judges. He did manage to push through prison reform legislation that allowed low-level offenders to be freed from jail. But aside from this, he was a lawbreaker who acted like a mob boss.

Yet, when the Supreme Court ruled against him, he felt betrayed since he appointed three Justices whom he thought he had in his pocket. He even wound up suing the Supreme Court—a meaningless and futile exercise since they would not rule against themselves if the court case ended in their jurisdiction.

His Inflexible Position on Guns

Trump was a complete adherent of the Second Amendment and did not push for any gun control legislation—despite the biggest mass shooting incident in Las Vegas, Nevada in 2017 that took 58 lives, wounded 422 persons, and injured 422 others in the rush to escape the gunfire. After several school shootings, he proposed arming teachers in schools, which would have created dangerous conditions for SWAT teams. And despite horrific shootings in El Paso, Texas; Dayton, Ohio; Odessa, Texas; New Orleans, Louisiana; Chicago, Illinois; and other cities, he never pushed for any legislation to restrict weapons, always being coached by the NRA. He only agreed to the banning of bump stocks, one of which was used in the deadly Las Vegas shooting.

His Concocted Conspiracies

Trump's twitter account became a source of falsehoods. He amplified disinformation as he campaigned for the presidency and for the four years that he was in office. He suggested that President Obama and Vice President Biden had the Seal Team killed because they botched the Osama bin Laden raid, and that bin Laden was still alive. As he campaigned for the 2016 election, he stated again that President Obama was not a United States citizen. In the 2020 election, he touted the same thing about Vice Presidential candidate Kamala Harris. He also claimed that Obama tapped his phone during the 2016 election.

Trump fanned the flames of extremists. After a Neo-Nazi rally in Charlottesville, Virginia in which a counter demonstrator was killed, he referred to the Nazis as "very fine people". In 2020, he told the right-wing group, the Proud Boys, to "stand back and stand by". His own presidential advisor, Stephen Miller, introduced racist views in speeches that he wrote for President Trump. Trump also catered to QAnon, which is a disinformation network and subscribed to the views of *Breitbart News*.

The most egregious declaration by Trump was that President Barack Obama had the government spy on him for political purposes. Trump made assertions, without providing any evidence in 2018, that it was done to help Hillary Clinton win the 2020 election. Trump further alleged that a counterintelligence operation into the Trump campaign had been running since 2015 and claimed that a FISA warrant was issued for this purpose. However, in 2019, the DOJ found no evidence to support this claim.

Trump and Education

Trump is not interested in making formal education affordable. Instead, he is promoting private charter schools that will create further divisions between students of means and those students who must attend public schools. He is not interested in science and engineering except for the knowledge to produce more lethal weapons. He is not interested in intelligence—the capacity to think clearly and objectively. He is only interested in having a society that obeys orders by forcing people to behave in a certain manner. His actions and words do not engender less violence in the world, something that is necessary for education to flourish in a meaningful way.

His aim appears to be of having an educational system that only serves to make students conform, to adjust and to fit into the prevailing system. He is not concerned with the cultivation of education for the long vision, but rather focuses on immediate gains through specialization that will produce more profits for the wealthy. He certainly does not act to provide better pay and teaching environments for teachers. He is only intent on arming them with weapons so that learning institutions will become armed camp centers.

Trump failed to enact any sweeping school choice policy that sends money to parents to help them pay for private and religious schools. But his administration found ways to expand federal support for religious schools and faith-based organizations at the Education Department. At the K-12 education level, he stopped enforcing a policy that had prohibited religious organizations from providing publicly funded services—such as tutoring, technology and counseling—in private schools. And he opened federal grants for charter schools to religiously affiliated organizations. At the end of his presidency, he released a 1776 report that excused slavery, justified the Three-fifths compromise and railed against "identity politics". He also celebrated the right to bear arms and called the anti-abortion movement as one of the nation's greatest reforms. He defended the country's founding fathers, many of whom owned slaves, by arguing that slavery was not a uniquely American evil and that it needed to be seen in a much broader perspective. In that context he objected to the critical race theory of the 1619 Project that was launched in 2020, which aimed to reframe the country's history by placing the consequences of slavery and the contributions of Black Americans at the very center of the United States' national narrative.

President Trump dismantled the Obama-era policies to curb abuses and that made it easier for student borrowers to obtain loan forgiveness. Borrowers seeking to have their student loans wiped out because of the misconduct of their college—such as misleading or deceiving students about their job prospects—had a tougher time proving their claims.

His Failure to Deal with Infrastructure

President Trump ran on the slogan of "Make America Great Again" because he was going to redo the infrastructure, which was in a deteriorating state. But he never got around to it, and the only structure that he managed to construct was his medieval fence. He even took money from the Pentagon to build some of the fence, and he forced a government shutdown when Congress would not appropriate any money for it. The shutdown lasted for 35 days until it started impacting the air traffic control system and commercial aviation when the airport controllers started calling in sick in large numbers, thus shutting down the commercial airline traffic. Only then did he cave in and sign a budget bill to restore government funding.

His Obsession with the ACA and Other Health Issues

Since the very beginning of his term, President Trump tried everything to do away with the ACA. He tried several times through Congress but failed each time. He tried by cutting funds away from the ACA but did not succeed in killing it. He tried through the courts and failed there also. He even tried through executive orders, but these were all rejected by the courts. He wanted to replace the ACA with his own plan, but he never unveiled his health care plan, simply because he didn't have one. He spent four years of his administration on a mission to destroy the ACA—merely because it had been enacted under the Obama administration.

Trump instituted a policy of working against the legalization of marijuana, He did very little to mitigate the opioid crisis in America. Trump had his Attorney General Jeff Sessions revert government policy back to "reefer madness" days. He rescinded the Cole memo that called for deprioritizing marijuana enforcement—even as 18 states liberalized their marijuana laws from 2018 to 2020, and where cannabis became legal in 36 states—even though the drug remained illegal at the federal level, despite of it being prescribed for medicinal purposes.

During the coronavirus pandemic crisis, he had governors bidding against each other for ventilators, personal protection equipment (PPE), and supplies. He did nothing to alleviate the shortage of staffs, ICU beds and life-saving equipment at hospitals. Many hospitals resorted to the sharing of ventilators among patients to handle the overwhelming number who needed respiratory assistance. They also made gowns out of robes, plastic sheets and other cloths, and staff members were forced to wear used masks and gloves. He even accused hospital people of stealing PPE and taking them home with them.

His Failed Economic Policies

The stock market climbed to record levels as the DOW surpassed 30,000 points. However, he fell short of what Presidents Obama and Clinton did while they were in office. He was also successful in pushing a tax cut, which mainly benefitted the corporations and rich Americans. He brought down unemployment levels to record low levels of about 3%—until the coronavirus pandemic hit and created an economic recession as a result of shutdowns of businesses. The resulting recession left more than 25 million unemployed and created a record filing of over 74.5 million claims over a span of 43 weeks.

The stimulus package of $2.4 trillion that he signed did not do enough to alleviate the situation, and subsequent attempts at passing another stimulus bill failed until the very end of his presidency when a $900 billion stimulus bill was passed that provided $600 checks to those who qualified. The stimulus package that was passed was insufficient and people were left with no money. Long food lines formed, and many tenants were evicted because they had no money for rent or mortgage payments.

Under the Trump administration, the federal government rolled out a series of employer-friendly rules and decisions. His Labor Department finalized an overtime rule that was notably weaker than that issued under the Obama administration, leaving millions of workers ineligible. The Trump rule applied to just 15% of full-time, salaried workers, and at least 8 million workers who would have been eligible for overtime pay became ineligible.

In the meantime, the national debt increased by over $7.8 trillion in the four years of his presidency to $27.8 trillion as he touted himself as "the king of debt".

Trump instituted tariffs on China that forced him to subsidize farmers with $48 billion as a result of China halting all agricultural product purchases from the United States. Even so, 25% of the farming community declared bankruptcy. He also placed tariffs on other countries, which resulted in higher prices for consumers in the United States. Trump opted out of the Transpacific Partnership with Far East nations. He tried to bring back manufacturing to the United States but in the process lost more jobs—especially after the coronavirus pandemic hit. Trump got the NAFTA agreement terminated and replaced it with a new agreement, United States-Mexico-Canada Agreement (USMCA), which was almost the same as the original NAFTA agreement.

Under Trump, the Agriculture Department scaled back the $60 billion SNAP program, the food support program for low-income Americans known as food stamps. He also made it more difficult for states to seek waivers for SNAP work requirements for adults who were not caring for children or other dependents. As a result, over 750,000 Americans lost their access to food. This created huge food lines when the coronavirus pandemic hit and left people without jobs and money.

The Endangerment of the Environment

President Trump embarked on creating more coal powered plants—the worst polluters in the world, labeling them as "clean coal" endeavors—and to promote the fossil fuel industry. He put tariffs on solar cells, claimed windmills killed thousands of birds and caused cancer, lifted restrictions on drilling offshore and in the ANWR, and cut back on earth monitoring satellite projects. He allowed asbestos-filled products in the United States despite the high incidence of mesothelioma cases as a known carcinogen. He withdrew much of the regulations concerning toxic chemicals, thus endangering those who handled and used these chemicals.

He accelerated oil and gas extractions and opened the coasts on the Atlantic and Pacific Oceans and federal lands to drilling—except for Florida where his Mar-a-Lago residence is located. He did not sign a treaty agreed to by 187 nations to halt the contamination of the earth by plastic materials. He killed NASA's carbon monitoring system of the planet. He had the EPA exempt 31 small oil refineries from rules that would require them to blend ethanol. He instructed the EPA to no longer approve labels warning that glyphosate is known to cause cancer, such as in the Monsanto Roundup weed killer product. He withdrew from the Paris Climate Accord that was signed by almost every nation in the world to combat global warming.

Trump placed a freeze on EPA grants and contracts and cut the budget of the EPA. He had the EPA roll back rules for oil and gas industry emissions of methane. He rolled back rules against air, water. and land pollution. He provided no funding for the California wildfires and said that they could be prevented by "raking the forests". Trump also signed an executive order diverting water to California farmers that went against California's water plan.

Trump released Alaska's Tongass National Forest from logging restrictions—America's largest national forest. He opened up Alaska to mining projects that threatened the wild salmon fisheries. The Trump administration rolled back clean water regulations, which placed limits on polluting chemicals that could be used near streams, wetlands, rivers, and other bodies of water. His border fence was built through the Organ Pipe Cactus National Monument. Bulldozers ripped through the most spectacular Sonoran Desert ecosystem on the planet. Endangered species, Native American sacred sites and protected wilderness were under immediate threat. Trump removed nearly 100 environmental restrictions and regulations that were intended to limit pollution, which allowed corporations to circumvent pollution restraints. Worst of all, he denied that global warming was happening, and he denigrated the science that supported it.

He was against solar power and placed a 30% tariff tax on imported solar cells. He was against wind turbines, and he forged ahead with the Keystone XL project for an oil pipeline project despite the many environmental objections, especially by Native Americans, as being capable of destroying the environment.

His Abject Failure to Deal with the Coronavirus

In January 2020, Trump was told of the deadly and highly contagious coronavirus by Chinese President Xi before any cases had occurred in the United States. President Trump did nothing, played down the virus—even calling it a hoax by the Democrats. When the first 15 cases were reported in the United States, he stated that it would disappear by April 2020. Instead, the coronavirus spread like wildfire as it hit the populous states of New York and California. By the time that he instituted a travel ban from China, over 40,000 people had come to the United States from China, many of whom were carriers of the disease. He also instituted a ban from Europe, but again too late as thousands of travelers from Europe infected New York and other areas in the Eastern United States.

The coronavirus pandemic brought all of Trump's incompetence into focus. He was not prepared to deal with the coronavirus, and he tried all his tactics of hiding it, blaming it on others, and mostly ignoring it. When the first case appeared in Washington state, he said that "it was only one case of a person coming in from China and that the United States had it under control". Even though he knew that the virus was deadly, he downplayed it, comparing it to the flu—and predicting "that it would go away when the weather warmed up". He even pushed quack coronavirus "cures" like the malaria drug hydroxychloroquine and injecting bleach. The consequences, of course, were deadly. He mocked masks and discredited the scientific community, including the respected Dr. Anthony Fauci.

After the virus increased in intensity across the United States, Trump set up a task force to deal with the coronavirus headed by Vice President Pence. However, after a few weeks, he lost interest in controlling the spread of the disease, and the task force eventually disbanded. As a result, 400,000 people died from the illness, with more than 24 million people becoming infected during his last year in office. He did create a "warp speed" project for a vaccine, but three independent drug companies produced a vaccine—none of which were funded by the "warp speed" project. Trump also withdrew the United States from WHO. The FDA and the CDC did approve of the Pfizer and Moderna vaccines for use in the United States, with shipments being sent out to all 50 states. However, he bungled the distribution of the vaccines by having no plan and not enough vaccine reserves.

Five presidents before him looked to Dr. Tony Fauci for advice on medical matters but Trump was the first to angrily dismiss the counsel that Dr. Fauci offered because it did not fit with his own poor instincts. This is because Trump's style of governing rejected facts and demanded that people see the world his way, that they live in his counterfactual reality. Trump will go down in history as a president who worsened the grief and tragedy of the most consequential pandemic in 100 years by being incapable of empathy, and who chose to remain cocooned in his White House bubble at a time when leadership would have mattered.

In March 2020, before the virus had become a serious problem, several underwear makers were pulled together to manufacture 650 million 3-ply masks—enough to send a packet of 5 to every household in America. But the plan was killed by the White House, something that could have saved thousands of lives and prevented millions of cases. In April 2020, when the CDC recommended that all Americans wear masks. President Trump stated that mask wearing was voluntary. He also forced the CDC to water down re-opening guidelines for businesses, schools, restaurants, and other facilities. He wanted less testing to be performed because it was causing an increasing number of coronavirus cases to be reported. He became a super spreader of the virus by holding political rallies without social distancing or mask requirements.

Trump was focused solely on economics and did not want states to shut down because he stated that "The cure cannot be worse than the problem". Because he did not take precautions, such as wearing a mask, President Trump contracted the coronavirus as did 40 of his immediate staff members. He was treated at the Walter Reed Hospital where he recovered with the administration of an experimental medical cocktail. He returned to the White House even though he was sick and contagious, but he did not wear a mask. He then embraced the idea of allowing the virus to spread unchecked until the point of "herd immunity" was attained.

In the middle of the pandemic, Trump announced that the United States would not participate in a global effort led by WHO to develop and distribute a coronavirus vaccine because the Trump administration said that it would not be constrained by the "corrupt" organization although more than 170 other countries were involved with WHO. He also cut United States funding to WHO. A report by the Lancet Commission found that four out of every ten deaths in the United States from the coronavirus could have been avoided. But Trump instead brough misfortune during his time in office although the situation was exacerbated by the poor public health infrastructure.

The Pfizer vaccine was approved for use in the United States as was the Moderna vaccine to prevent the coronavirus. However, neither of these companies receive any funding from his "Project Warp speed". Poor planning for logistics resulted in the virus shipments being held up. And he never took any responsibility for the failure to adequately handle the outbreak of the coronavirus, which ultimately spread like wildfire in the entire United States. Soon after his inauguration, he dismantled the epidemic group that had been created by the Obama administration to deal with virus outbreaks, which it did with the Ebola virus. Trump mostly ignored the coronavirus pandemic and left no plan behind for either the distribution or the administration of the vaccine. The only truthful statement that he made concerning the virus was this: "There is going to be a whole lot of deaths". Considering what he promised in his inaugural speech in which he said that "the American carnage stops right now", it stands as an utter failure of his leadership, given what has happened with the coronavirus pandemic under his watch. When he finished his term, more than 400,000 Americans had died from the coronavirus and more than 23 million had contracted it.

The Mueller Investigation

In 2017, Mueller empaneled a grand jury in Washington, D.C. as part of his investigation. The grand jury has the power to subpoena documents, require witnesses to testify under oath, and issue indictments for targets of criminal charges if probable cause is found. The grand jury has issued several subpoenas to those involved in the Trump campaign. In 2017, Trump reportedly told his lawyer McGahn to fire Mueller, but was persuaded to back off from this course of action. He was anguished as he exclaimed, "I'm fucked".

In April 2019, the Mueller investigation completed its report. However, Attorney General William Barr only released a 4-page summary of the 448-page report, which exonerated the President and stated that there was no collusion. Later, he released a heavily redacted report to Congress and the public, with almost 1,000 redactions. Thus, Barr had the final Mueller report redacted such that no charges were ever brought against Trump.
The redacted report, nevertheless, detailed ten events in which Mueller's team stated that Trump may have attempted to obstruct justice, and was only saved from being indicted by the failure of his aides to carry out his orders or accede to his requests. After the Mueller redacted report was released, the White House released a transcript of Trump's written answers to questions that Mueller posed to him. Trump could not remember or recall anything in his answers.

Several subpoenas were issued to obtain his financial information, but none succeeded. He was charged with violating the Emoluments Clause of the Constitution with his private business companies. President Trump also fired several top officials, including the FBI Director James Comey for allegedly investigating him for his Russian election interference in 2016 and Attorney General Sessions because he recused himself from the Russia investigation.

Military and Foreign Affairs Failures

President Trump pushed through almost $3 trillion in defense budgets. But he alienated NATO allies as he sought relationships with Russia and China instead. He met with the premier of North Korea in an attempt to denuclearize the country, but he failed in the ensuing negotiations. During that time North Korea continued to develop its nuclear and ballistic missile programs.

He tried unsuccessfully to negotiate with the Taliban in Afghanistan to execute a withdrawal of United States troops. In a hasty move, Trump released thousands of imprisoned terrorists to create a deal with the Taliban. He imposed new sanctions on Iran and pulled out of the nuclear deal, thus allowing Iran to proceed on their quest for a nuclear weapon. He even asked the Pentagon for options to militarily strike Iran's nuclear facilities. He stayed silent when it was disclosed that Russia had paid the Taliban to kill American soldiers.

He did kill the Iranian Revolutionary leader, which resulted in Iran firing missiles into Baghdad, seriously injuring over 100 United States troops with concussions and other brain injuries, calling them "headaches". He also killed the head of ISIS. But he pulled American troops that were protecting the Kurds, who had been allies in the Iraq War, leaving them defenseless and open to attacks by the Turkish Army. He did send a missile salvo at Syria after they chemically attacked their own citizens but did nothing else to stop their civil war.

President Trump dissed the military by calling those who had served in WWII as "suckers and losers". And when the United States departments and Pentagon were hacked by Russia, he remained silent even though it endangered national security. Trump behaved mostly as if he were compromised by Russia and thus never criticized Russia or its leader Vladimir Putin in the four years that he was in office.

Trump did create a new Space Force that would be a distinct and separate military organization. However, he continuously denigrated his generals who he considered to be not aggressive enough, especially against ISIS and other insurgents. He also instituted a modernized nuclear arsenal and withdrew the United States from the Open Skies Treaty—and then dismantled the two specialized Boeing aircraft that were used for this purpose.

Trump threatened Venezuela but did not intervene militarily to depose of its dictator. He continued the participation of the United States with Saudi Arabia in the Yemen War. He was able to get a peace for Israel with some of the Arab nations, including the initiation of diplomatic relations and the establishment of embassies. But he moved the United States Embassy from Tel Aviv to Jerusalem, thus infuriating the Palestinians. Trump alienated the countries in South America and cut off aid to Central American countries.

The Constant Attack on the Media

From the very beginning of his candidacy, Trump attacked the media and labeled them as "the enemy of the people". He labeled the various news reports about him as being "fake news" to dangerously undermine truth and consensus, which served to create a deeply divided nation. Trump showed a disdain for the press and even tried to place restrictions on the press. He belittled reporter's questions, he had the DOJ investigate reporter's sources of information, he called for changes in libel laws to punish reporting that he didn't like, and frequently ended press briefings for long periods of time.

Trump devoted large amounts of time at his rallies denouncing the press and encouraging the boisterous crowds to react, He regularly pointed to the assembled group of reporters, photographers and videographers in the press section, prompting people in the crowd to turn around and shout expletive-laden words at them. It also led to news organizations receiving threats against them. And as the pandemic, social events and economic hardships emerged, he doubled down on the intensity of his attacks on the media, especially as the 2020 election drew near. He never stopped retaliating against the media and only embraced news outlets like FOX News who were mostly friendly towards him.

Using the Presidency for Gain

Trump treated the presidency like his own private business. He practiced personal corruption to funnel taxpayer money into his pocket. He openly solicited money through his hotels and golf courses from both domestic and foreign interests. He visited his properties over 320 time during the 4 years to play golf—even though during the campaign he said that he would be too busy to play golf because he would be "working his ass off". Secret Service personnel and staff who accompanied him on these golfing excursions had to pay to stay at his resorts at taxpayer expense for room rentals and meals—as well as for golf cart rentals and accessories. President Trump diverted millions of dollars from Republican donors. His hotels became attractions for lobbyists. There were also abuses of the Hatch Act by some of his staff. Even at his acceptance speech at the RNC convention, the event was held at the White House with staff being employed to support the activities. Trump also violated the Emoluments Clause of the Constitution with his hotel in Washington, D.C., which was against the agreement that he signed in acquiring the property before he became President.

Trump Has No Relationship to the World

Trump idealizes and escapes into a world of future fantasy rather than dealing with the present reality. His mindset manifests itself as a process of isolation through which he talks a great deal about subjects that satisfy his ego at the moment. He only seeks gratification and avoids any disturbances that upset his vanity. He builds resistance against everyone and seals himself behind a mental wall that encloses him in his secure perch.

Trump promotes nationalism with his "America First" credo, thinking that he can create world peace. But, in doing so, he further isolates himself from what exists in the world: sorrow, war, famine, destruction, agony, decay, disease, misery, and disruption. He seeks power through which he can dominate others via a bureaucratic regime that runs based on economic, military, industrial and technological structures. Thus, he has no affection for the world, and he operates without any empathy for others.

His patriotic spirit lies in identifying himself with his country, and by building walls of resistance against other countries. He is in perennial conflict and lives continually in a state of contradiction, telling lies upon lies in a never-ending manner. His reference to God is merely an identification with something bigger and is solely a lust for greater power—a desire that has a motive of controlling everything and everyone. His spiritual nature is nil since he plays golf on most weekends rather than attend any church, participate in any service, meditate, or engage in introspection. He has stated that his favorite book is the Bible, but he has probably never read it. He even had police disperse protesters so that he could be in front of St. Michael's Church in Washington, D.C., holding an upside-down bible with his right hand in the air—a photo op with no clear purpose, except maybe for a divine mandate or as an act of defiance.

He has no empathy for others, and he has no sympathy for the plight of people across the globe. People are merely objects to him, to be used for his objectives—and to be discarded when they no longer meet his aims.

Domestic Strife

Domestically, many disturbances occurred as a result of several Blacks being killed by the police. He responded by sending unbadged and masked military people into cities like Portland, Oregon and Seattle, Washington to arrest protestors who were held without bond. He supported White Supremacists and criticized organizations such as BLM. He also defended Confederate statues. He was against the renaming of military bases that are named after Confederate generals. He even wanted to invoke the Insurrection Act to send troops to the cities to quell the disturbances, but the Secretary of Defense refused to comply. He also attacked LGBT people and banned them from the military.

The Trump administration rolled back policies that he denounced as "social engineering". The Fair Housing Rule was scrapped, and he withheld housing funds from cities by making it harder for plaintiffs to claim intentional housing discrimination. In addition, the Consumer Financial Protection Bureau gave small banks an exemption from data collection requirements that help track racial discrimination in the mortgage market. The agency also dramatically cut back on enforcing fair lending laws.

Voting Interference

Trump hired a new Postal Administrator, Louis DeJoy, to sabotage the Post Office. DeJoy removed mailboxes, dismantled hundreds of sorting machines, cut overtime and made changes to slow down the processing of mail—all in an effort to affect mail-in ballots. And even after the outcome of the 2020 election was determined, he attempted a coup by filing over 60 lawsuits in the courts to overturn the election results—all of which he lost except for one. He demanded recounts in some states that he lost, claiming voter fraud. He even asked Republican legislators to overturn the election results in their states and appoint Electors that would vote for him instead—an unheard of attack on the democracy of the United States.

The Electoral College vote finally ended his attempt to subvert the democratic process involved in an election. When all those efforts failed, he looked to January 6, 2021, when a joint session of Congress would meet to formally count the Electoral College results, seeing it as another opportunity to try and thwart the democratic process. Since losing the election, Trump has repeated that the election was stolen from him over 200 different times. He even asked the Georgia Secretary of State to overturn the results of the election by having him "find" 11,780 votes—even after Georgia had already twice certified the voting results that showed that Biden had won.

Trump supported the Ninja Warriors who did a recount of the votes in Maricopa County, Arizona, with the result being that they affirmed that Biden won. He also had recounts done in a few states, again none of which overturned the results. As a last resort, he encouraged the sending of fake electors in five key states that he lost, hoping that Mike Pence would reject the legitimate Electoral votes in those states and ask for an investigation.

With the White House documents that were handed over to the House Select Committee in January 2022, it was discovered that Trump had a draft executive order that commanded the Secretary of Defense to order the Pentagon to seize the Dominican voting machines in the seven key states that he lost. An assessment would then be made by a special counsel selected by Trump 60 days from the commencement of the operation, pushing the date into February 2021, well beyond the inauguration date of January 20, 2021. He even had plans to appoint his lawyer, Sidney Powell, as the head of the special counsel to carry out this plan.

His Attempted Coup by Inciting a Riot

Trump summoned his supporters to a "Stop the Steal" rally at the White House lawn on January 6, 2021. He told them, "Be there. It will be wild". They came to Washington, D.C. because Trump told them to. He wanted to stay in power so much that his most egregious act in a desperate move was when he incited a huge crowd of his supporters, at his request, to march to the Capitol building when the Electoral College vote count for Joe Biden was being officially certified by Congress. He gave an incendiary speech, exhorting his followers "to use strength and to fight like hell or else they would no longer have a country". He also said that he would march with them, which he didn't. About 2,000 of his minions who were in attendance then marched to the Capitol building, pushed through barriers that had been set up around the Capitol building and stormed the Capitol building, entering the House and the Senate floors in a violent event of insurrection.

One Capitol policeman was killed and only the sequestering of lawmakers prevented any gross bloodshed, which would have occurred if the mob had gotten hold of any of the lawmakers. Instead of calling them to stop, or ordering the National Guard to quell the riot, he told them that "he loved them" and praised them as "very special people." He later defended them by saying that "These are the things and events that happen when a sacred landslide election victory is so unceremoniously and viciously stripped away". Not once in 3 hours of the mayhem did Trump inquire as to the safety of Pence and the lawmakers. President Trump had actually wanted the military to take over the Congress, but 10 former Secretary of defense members intervened and stated their opposition in a letter to the Pentagon,

His attempted coup was deliberate, and he had it all planned out. When he incited his supporters to march to the Capitol building, he was expecting them to go in there with guns and to start shooting the lawmakers. House Speaker Nancy Pelosi and Vice President Mike Pence were in harm's way and would probably have been killed—and he knew that. Then, no certification would have taken place and he could declare martial law, thus remaining as President. But his minions were not militias and so his plot failed. Although they did some damage, and killed a Capitol officer, as a whole they were not astute enough to do anything else—even though Rudy Giuliani had egged them on to commit violence by saying that it was a "trial by combat".

It came very close to being a bloody coup for if any Democratic Congressmen had been captured, they would probably have been murdered. The saving grace was that the lawmakers were sequestered. Trump took relish in watching it on TV and he refused to call the National Guard as he did not care at all about the safety of the lawmakers nor of his Vice President whom he had instructed to reject the certified Electoral votes. The rioters even wanted to hang Pence and erected gallows outside the Capitol building.

In an expletive-laden phone call with House Republican leader Keith McCarthy while the Capitol building was under attack, President Trump said that "the rioters cared more about the election results than McCarthy did". McCarthy insisted that the rioters were

Trump's supporters and begged President Trump to call them off. A shouting match ensued between the two men and a furious McCarthy told the President that the rioters were breaking into his office through the windows, and he asked President Trump, "Who the fuck do you think you are talking to"? Even Ivanka Trump and Donald Trump, Jr. asked Trump to intervene—to no avail.

Trump had no intention of calling off the rioters even as lawmakers were pleading with him to intervene—a dereliction of his Presidential duty. He was holding an insurrection against the United States for his own personal gain. It was Vice President Pence who finally called the Army Secretary who then authorized the National Guard to go in to quell the insurrection. Eight people died as a result of the riot, including 3 Capitol policemen and 140 law enforcement officers were injured. Only later did President Trump make a video denouncing his supporters—but only to save his own skin from being prosecuted. But he never called the National Guard.

His refusal to acknowledge defeat combined with his following of "patriots" drawn from the ranks of extremists, created a toxic and dangerous environment for the country. By his own words and actions Trump hated losing and would not own up to it when it happened. Democracy and human life were of no concern to him. His only aim was to disrupt the certification process to maintain his grip on power. Without showing any empathy, Trump never acknowledged the death of the Capitol policeman who was killed by the mob. Without showing any sympathy, Trump never offered any condolences to the family of the Capitol policeman. And only reluctantly the White House flag was flown at half-mast—but only for a single day after 3 days had passed.

If the coup had succeeded, for example, by some lawmakers getting killed or injured, then he would have declared martial law and he would have remained in power since Joe Biden would not be certified as President. It was a deliberate attempt to overthrow the government because Trump had meetings with his associates before January 6, 2021, in which the plans for the event were made.

Impeachment

In 2019, Trump became the third President to be impeached. The House Democrats submitted their first legal filing that outlined their case for removing President Trump from office, arguing that the Senate should convict him for abuse of power and obstruction of Congress. In a brief, the House impeachment managers made their case, claiming that Trump improperly pressured Ukraine to publicly announce investigations of his political rivals, including former Vice President Joe Biden and his son, Hunter Biden. Democrats asserted that the Trump administration withheld $400 million in military aid in a bid to force Ukraine to launch the investigations. However, the Senate failed to convict Trump on both charges in the trial that was held in 2020 although there was one Republican, Mitt Romney, who did vote to convict him on one of the charges.

In 2021, Trump became the first President to be impeached twice. He was charged with inciting the riot that took place at the Capitol building on January 6, 2021, when Congress was counting the Electoral votes to certify the win by President-elect Joe Biden. The charge was incitement of insurrection for his act of whipping up his most ardent followers into a deadly mob who then ransacked the Capitol building, forcing lawmakers to evacuate both the Senate and House floors. However, the Senate once again failed to convict Trump—even though 7 Republicans voted to convict him.

His Role as a Russian Asset

In all his dealings with Russia, including several talks with Vladimir Putin, Trump never criticized Russia or Putin during his campaign, or in his four years as President. As Colonel Alexander Vindman stated after the first impeachment trial, "Trump was Putin's useful idiot". The *Guardian* published a story in which a Russian KGB major, Yuir Shvets, stated that Donald Trump was cultivated as a Russian asset since 1977. Craig Unger cited this source in his book *American Kompromat* in which he explored the relationship between Moscow and Trump.

When Trump married his first wife, Ivana, in 1977, he became the target of a spying operation that was overseen by Czechoslovakia's intelligence service in cooperation with the KGB. In 1980, Trump developed the Grand Hyatt Hotel and bought 200 television sets from Joy-Lud Electronics whose owner was controlled by the KGB and who used him as a spotter agent for a potential asset. In 1987, Trump and Ivana visited Russia where he was flattered by operatives who told him he should go into politics. The KGB had collected a lot of information on his personality and understood that he was extremely vulnerable intellectually and psychologically—and that he was prone to flattery, a trait that was perfect for exploitation. Trump also took out an ad criticizing America's foreign defense policy, which was greeted with much jubilation in Russia. After he returned to the United States, Trump began exploring a run for President.

In 2013, Trump held the Miss Universe Beauty Pageant in Moscow. When he was asked if he had a personal relationship with Putin, Trump answered in the affirmative. The 2013 pageant became a focal point for the simultaneous investigations, led by special counsel Robert Mueller and the congressional committees, into whether associates of Trump colluded with Russian officials to help them win the 2016 presidential election. There were also allegations as documented in the dossier compiled by British agent Christopher Steele about Trump's private conduct behind closed doors at the Ritz-Carlton hotel during his 2013 stay in Moscow, including a "golden shower" sexual interlude that was put on for his pleasure—and which compromised him.

During the campaign in 2015, Trump was actively involved in having a Trump Tower built in Moscow, with the penthouse being given to Putin for free as well as with a spa that would be designed by Trump's daughter, Ivanka Trump. Trump was repeatedly asked whether he had any involvement with Russia and he denied it. His lawyer, Michael Cohen, lied for him too even though he was directly involved in the negotiations. Later, Cohen recanted and said that Trump was negotiating up until the time that he was elected as President. Supposedly, Ivanka Trump paid a visit to Moscow and even sat in Putin's presidential chair—a sign of the chumminess of the relationship for the potential deal.

In 2016, when Trump finally ran a full campaign and won the presidential election, his campaign and transition team had at least 272 known contacts with Russia-linked operatives. The Russians helped to elect Trump with their disinformation and election interference. The Mueller investigation never followed up on this because it was centered on crime-related issues. Also, during his presidency, Trump criticized NATO, much to Russia's delight.

His Insatiable Desire

For all his life, Trump has been driven by desire that has centered on power, wealth, and sex. His vast accumulations of real estate, his many ventures into businesses and his dealings with banks have all been about money. His many girlfriends and three wives indicate an insatiable lust. And his striving after the presidency again denotes the ultimate pinnacle in his quest to be the most powerful person on the planet—but this time with vengeance and spite.

Trump's pattern of desire has been put together through greed. His drive to achieve success has made him very competitive, and it has caused him to act without any restraints all his life. It is a desire that has manifested itself by the creation of an image about himself. But in pursuing materialism, it has created much disorder in his life. Although he doesn't smoke, drink, or take drugs, he still has an attachment to things— and to women. His restless desire to conquer women sexually has restricted his social growth and has limited his capacity for expressing emotion—except for his angry outbursts. Even with his boundless energy that he displays, his capacity to expand his mental awareness and to express his feelings in a conscious manner has been limited.

His desire for women is an unsatisfied quest to attain bliss. He may experience this satisfaction with his sexual encounters, but these are fleeting moments in his life, and they achieve nothing but momentary gratification. The sexual encounters are probably more of a refuge for him rather than providing him with a path toward emotional growth. He can lust after women everlastingly, but it won't give him the inner joy that he probably would like to experience. That is why he seeks adulation—to fill the void that is in his life because deep inside he is a very unhappy person who has sacrificed his happiness for the petty actions of anger, hate, jealousy, spitefulness, and possessiveness.

Trump's Mind is in the Past

Trump's patented phrase of "Make America Great Again" shows that he is fixated with the past. He would like to transform the country back to the days of oil monopolies, giant steel plants and huge coal producing mines, with huge corporate banks funding all these activities. In his mind, everything was wonderful before all of the civil rights activities, women's rights pursuits and social changes took place. He claims to be a history buff, but some of his heroes have blemished records. He also has a distorted view of history—probably because he doesn't read any books about it.

Trump takes actions based on his beliefs about the world. His promotion of the Christian belief system pits him against the Islamic belief system—and thus creates conflict. His adherence to the Anglo-Saxon cultural white supremacy puts him at odds with cultures of the rest of the world. Rather than perceive what is, he acts on images in his mind that are based on memory and knowledge. He does not observe reality as it is, but rather views events and people from a perspective that he has accumulated throughout the years.

As Trump moves further along in life, his mind is fragmenting as he remains fixed in his beliefs. He is struggling to avoid stagnation, but his level of frustration keeps increasing with time as events unfold. He has no real understanding of people—other than sizing them up according to his standards—and he regards people merely as a means to his ends since he only wants them to conform to his way of thinking. He wants people to work together although mainly by the use of threats, through inducement of fear, with punishment for those who do not cooperate, and via incentives of rewards for those who toe the line. Yet, his mind will continue to decline as long as it is caught up in a web that is anchored to the past.

The prime example of this adherence to the past is his concoction that the 2020 election was stolen from him. After all this time, despite several recounts and many court cases, he is still fixated on the imaginary notion that it was a fraudulent election. He will not admit defeat because being a loser is anathema to him.

It is All About Image for Trump

Trump has an image of himself that he has built up over the years. That is why he can't stand to be criticized because it goes against who he thinks he is. It is an image that has been built from the memory of his various experiences in which he has managed to survive, especially regarding his finances. It is an image in which he sees himself as a wealth-producing individual who has emerged relatively unscathed in his many adversarial businesses. It is also an image of a self-styled playboy who thinks that women love him—no matter what—and that he can do anything that he likes to them, such as his utterance of "You can grab them by the pussy". All of it is a theatrical performance that is meant to sway people.

In his narcissistic self, Trump goes after everything that he projects from his vanity. When he owned an airline service, he installed marble fixtures, plush carpets, and leather seats rather than satisfying the customers with what they wanted, which was flexible, inexpensive, and reliable flights. When he owned casinos, he made them into glitzy palaces with all the bells and whistles instead of concentrating on running them efficiently. When he ran a television show called "The Apprentice" the whole emphasis was always to glorify his business acumen.

When Trump does something he expects people to give him their approbation. As he gets older, he wants to be acknowledged by many people, especially for doing things for the sake of the country. But underneath all of this, he is doing it to gain recognition to satisfy his feeling of pride. That is why he has his name emblazoned on everything—so that people will recognize him as a great person. But all that he is cultivating is a hollow image, full of bluster and snobbery.

Trump wants to emulate the great leaders of the past, to imitate their behaviors, and to try to become like them. But he will be disillusioned because he will always be envious of those who have experienced greater accolades than he has. He wants to be very famous, to increase his fame by having his picture appear everywhere: in newspapers, magazines, television, the Internet, and the new social media such as Facebook, Twitter, YouTube, and Instagram. He probably even wishes that replicas of himself would be portrayed in paintings and statues. In his self-centered ego, he wants to be glorified like a king.

His Lack of Sensitivity

Trump has referred to women with demeaning names such as pigs. He is insensitive to disabled people and he even wanted to hide amputees from participating in parades. He says things that only serve to separate people, incites violence with his rhetoric—such as what happened on January 6, 2021—and he creates disharmony with his actions. He cares little about the environment, animal life or sea life, he denigrates everyone around him, and he offends people with his crass remarks. He has separated families, denied entry to people seeking asylum, and disregarded people by minimizing the loss of life by natural disasters like what happened in Puerto Rico after a devastating hurricane. The only time that he purportedly showed a humanitarian interest was when people were attacked with chemical weapons in Syria. But his response was only one of retaliation by bombing.

There is No Love in His Heart

Although Trump likes to say the words "I love you" to his crowds at his rallies, he doesn't really mean it. Someone who loves does not deport people indiscriminately, separate children from their parents, disparages those who are different, and refers to Nazis, racists, and thugs as "very fine people". He only brings forth hostility with his harsh and indifferent attitude towards people. At best, if it can be referred to in this manner, he only loves himself. But it is pure narcissism—not love. His relationships are mostly geared to the performance of a project, a goal to be attained, or a person to be conquered. Love to Trump consists solely of a mental image of a romantic ideal. But, as soon as the situation becomes inadequate, boring, or he loses interest in it, he moves to somebody else with a new fantasy, which is totally based on sex—not love.

His Lack of Compassion

When calling the widows of slain soldiers, Trump is at a loss for words to express his condolences—even once saying that "he knew what he signed up for". When he speaks about the various shootings that have taken place, he displays no emotion, and instead focuses on gun rights, the Second Amendment, and on further arming citizens. When he talks about abortion, he has no regard for the welfare and rights of women. When he despises Muslims and bars them from entering the country, he shows no sympathy for them. Trump fought against Native Americans when he was in the casino business, he has made several discriminatory statements about African Americans and their intelligence, he has offended the Mexican culture with his inflammatory accusations of them being the cause of crime and drug smuggling, and all throughout his adult life he has treated poor and disadvantaged people with disdain, calling them "losers" and "lowlifes".

Trump as the Self

Trump touts his IQ, his education, his business smarts, and his military knowledge—even though he never served a day in the service of his country, avoiding the draft by 5 deferments and then getting disqualified by "bone spurs"—something that doesn't seem to bother him when he plays golf. He views himself as a great real estate developer and as a wealthy entrepreneur. He has published books about how he does deals and how he manages to stay on top. His name is his symbol, which he displays in a grandiose manner to denote his wealth. It is all about himself.

Trump says that he is the only one who can save the world: that "he alone can fix it". He is the idealist of nationalism who promotes peace—not through diplomacy—but with the threat of nuclear annihilation. He uses words and expressions in meaningless ways as they relate to things, events, processes, and people. He offers panaceas to induce people to follow him solely on the basis of faith in himself and what he says. But his verbal assertions do not bring about clarity and are merely repetitive phrases that are mostly lies. He quotes false solutions to basic human problems that betray the truth about reality.

Trump wants people to conform to his version of brotherhood, which is only a cover for his intent of separating people. And in every crisis that he is involved in, he only acts to protect himself—because that is what matters to him. He responds to everything according to his well-established patterns of thought. He exercises his power to provide gratification in his quest for security, and to hide the fear about being discovered as to who he really is.

Trump does not exemplify leadership, he does not uplift people, he is certainly not a model of spirituality, and he only voices "thoughts and prayers" in the aftermath of shootings in the workplace, religious institutions, and schools. His choices about dealing with fundamental problems are based on personal reward, pleasure, achievement, or justification.

Trump resists everything and takes no advice from anyone because he is guided by a desire to dominate others. As he goes from idea to idea, and from interest to interest, he creates resistance, conflict, chaos, and friction by undermining others. He blames everyone else when things do not work, when projects fail, or when events do not happen according to what he wanted or expected.

Trump compares, evaluates, and judges people, acts in tyrannical ways, and portrays himself as the great champion of liberty—especially regarding the ownership of weapons. But he is a con man and a cheat who only thinks about himself as he tries to generate the best images about his presence in the world.

Trump and Authority

Trump uses authority to dominate others so that he can pretend to provide security and well-being to everyone. But in being authoritative, he is destroying freedom. He plays the same themes over and over again, hoping that his use of repetitiveness will lead to people not being able to discern the truth. His rhetoric dulls the minds of his followers who blindly accept what he says without expressing any doubts. He is an actor on a stage who spouts ideas that are not based on reality. He casts a shadow on what is going on with his sensationalism that has no purpose behind it other than to make people believe him—and hence to hide the truth.

Trump admires dictators and envies them because they can do whatever they want without any consequences. He probably secretly wishes that he could have absolute power so that he could rule the country without having to answer to anyone. He despises laws and regulations, and only uses them when it is to his advantage to do so. He fires people on a whim, and then criticizes them after they are gone. He is very vindictive, and never forgets people who made fun of him, always seeking to get revenge in some manner. Pursuing authority comes from the disorder that he generates in his life, such that he seeks to control and direct everything to counter the disturbances in his life.

In asserting his authority, Trump only manages to create more conflict between people. There is no wisdom in doing things with authority and acting with authority in all matters shows only a lack of intelligence—and a denial of freedom for others. His use of authority only makes problems worse since there can be no compromise, especially when he uses intimidation and suppression though the threat of lawsuits against those who seek to counter him—in which he has filed about 3,500 lawsuits. He only wants submission, acceptance, loyalty, and imitation. He is trying to control everybody to go in a certain direction without knowing where he himself is going.

His Lack of Responsibility

Although Trump never accepts responsibility for what happens, he is still subject to the consequences of his actions. He has totally given up responsibility for his financial fiascos, for his economic actions that have had an adverse effect on a number of people, except for the rich, and for his behavior of shifting the blame to others for events that unravel as a result of his actions. Clearly, the situations that continue to manifest themselves as time goes on are a direct consequence of his behavior and actions. Thus, like a puppet on a string, he is at the total effect of what happens in his life, and all that occurs is that he is left with unresolved problems and failed purposes.

To Trump every business venture is a game of profit or loss, regardless of what results, such as layoffs, bankruptcies, or plant closings. He fails to see the hardships that are caused because he has no responsibility. He views war as a matter of "winning" regardless of the destruction, loss of life, depletion of resources or erosion of life support systems that ensue. He even spouted off that since, "we have nuclear weapons, then why don't we use them". No matter how much effort Trump does in any undertaking, he will always be mired in an endless struggle to make things work while not assuming any accountability for his actions.

His Use of Language

Trump's use of language—which was done mostly through tweets—is a very different way to convey his message. However, with his rants, raves, and rages, he has managed to alienate people by altering the language context from its common usage. His hypnotic statements when he speaks at rallies are meant to cause people to behave like robots. These utterings are dangerous because they are attacks on people, organizations, countries, cultures, and on society. And because of their confrontational nature, his words are liable to set off people who are mentally unbalanced.

Trump's oratory is deliberate and strategic, even though it is the disjointed output of a disordered mind. He uses language to create a brand for himself—one that leverages a feeling of strength, a sense of determination, and an impression that he alone can get the job done. Trump's explosive noun phrases, self-interruptions, departures from the theme, flashes of memory and side remarks are symptomatic of a person with a concentration problem. He uses hyperbole, repetition, and intensifiers. He also employs directness but suffers from sentence fragments, digressions, elementary grade-level utterances and segues. For him, it is all about sales talk.

Thus, many of his speeches are characterized by broken sentences and bizarre asides. They are not sustained arguments but rather a mishmash of disjointed statements that don't combine into something greater—again, a product of a disordered mind. He rallies his audiences through an impassioned, targeted conversation, even if it is one-sided and doesn't follow a clear narrative. Instead, he uses simple phrases like "Make America Great Again", "Build the Wall" and "Fake News". Many of Trump's catchphrases, such as "Believe me" and "Many people are saying", are versions of sales techniques, especially since he has over 50 years of experience as a salesman. Yet, Trump does not display any linguistic sophistication as most of his rhetoric is banter.

The Drama of Trump

Trump creates drama in response to any threat to his survival. He does this according to a pattern that he has established over the years by getting attention in the hopes of eliciting sympathy for his woes. It is an appeal that is made in an attempt to entice others to join in his cause and to elicit agreement. His communication is intended to con people into believing what he says. It does not represent any meaningful sharing, especially of his life. On the contrary, it is dealing with others in a negative context. By dramatizing everything, he avoids taking responsibility for his mistakes.

This was especially true during the last few weeks of his presidency. Trump posted or reposted over 100 messages on Twitter lashing out at the results of an election that he lost. He mentioned the coronavirus pandemic only four times—and even then, just to assert that he was right about the outbreak and that the experts were wrong.

Moody and sometimes depressed, Trump barely showed up to work, ignoring the health and economic crises afflicting the nation and largely clearing his public schedule of meetings unrelated to his desperate bid to rewrite history, especially the 2020 election results. He fixated on rewarding friends, purging the disloyal and punishing a growing list of perceived enemies—as well as issuing a raft of pardons to protect himself and his allies. His rage and detached-from-reality refusal to concede defeat showed him defiantly clinging to power—rather than on his way to exile. He spent the last few days conjuring up an attempted coup in an effort to subvert democracy and replace it with an autocracy.

To the bitter end, Trump did not call his victorious opponent, Joe Biden, and did not invite him to the White House for the traditional postelection visit. Trump also did not attend Joe Biden's inauguration, as he refused to participate in the peaceful transfer of power. And since that time, he has turned on his own party, angry that some Republicans have refused to accept his baseless claims and overturn the will of the voters. And most probably in the future, he will rant further rages and find new targets for his wrath.

His Lack of Integrity

Trump possesses no integrity since for the most part he is engaged in being at odds with everyone. The lack of integrity means that he functions by spreading falsehoods, by saying one thing and doing another, by promising people the moon and then reneging on what he said he was going to do, and by expressing himself in a manner that obfuscates the situations at hand. He is not interested in making a difference as his whole perspective is one of aggrandizing himself at every turn. Most of what he does is not relevant to people's well-being as it is all based on his penchant for making money.

Trump is obsessed with money, and he has traded off everything to attain it, including love, health, happiness, and satisfaction. Since money controls his actions, especially when he runs into money problems, he strives to hide his financial dealings, and instead weaves a tale about his success in the financial world. Making money to Trump represents pleasure and it is the most important activity in his life. He uses money as a means of measuring his success, and thus everything that he does is geared towards accumulating more of it through slick and clever schemes that have no integrity.

He Is Not Interested in Helping Others

Trump considers helping others as a waste of time. He is cynical and sarcastic, and he considers any effort to help people as a foolish action. All that he manages to do is to create a wall of separation to protect himself from any betrayal or harm. He conceals his emotions—except those of anger and frustration—and he defends his actions by stating that "he has no choice" but to pursue those endeavors that he wants. He purports to help others, but his actions show otherwise, especially with regard to natural disasters. He is only interested in how these events will affect the budget, and even overstates the amount of help that he provides.

He Has No Desire to Learn

Trump does not read books, cannot digest lengthy discussions on subjects, rarely sees films, and spends most of his time watching television news shows. He claims to operate through his "gut feelings" with respect to choices that he makes. However, this does not mean that he is keenly attentive, but rather that he displays his compulsive behavior, which is based on competitiveness. He expresses the worst possible scenarios to get people to be afraid in order to have them kotow to his divisive rhetoric. He merely wants to produce a resistance to change, which is not a movement of learning new ways of doing things. By doing so he damages society by distorting the truth with his "alternate realities".

He Only Acknowledges Those Who Support Him

An acknowledgement by Trump is reserved only for those who totally support him. Otherwise, he doesn't recognize people for their accomplishments. And as soon as they fall out of favor with him, he no longer appreciates them—even after they have provided valuable service to him. He has an inability to acknowledge someone without any reservation, so it becomes more of an exercise of a condescending evaluation of them. More than anything, he hates it when someone else is acknowledged instead of him for some activity that was done. As always, he wants to be recognized and acknowledged for all the things that he does—no matter how trivial they may be.

His Poor Decision Making

Trump's methods of decision making were probably formed in his early years and are related to the incidents in his life that shaped his outlook. He is rooted in having approval for everything that he does. He always has to "win" at all costs. He proceeds on the basis that he is always right, and he tries to manipulate all the circumstances to fit this assumption. Thus, he is not humble, shy, or retiring as he arrogantly constructs situations that are always win-lose scenarios. As such he winds up with an emptiness that manifests itself in pettiness and mediocrity. His decisions are not based on perception or observation. Rather, they stem from years of having it his way. Hence, his decisions result in confrontations because there is no give-and-take. This is how he ran his companies: with absolute power to do anything that he wanted, and with no room for anyone to question his decisions.

Trump is Full of Contradictions

Trump is in a constant fury of denial and assertion, which means that he is in a state of contradiction, striving for what he wants to be rather than accepting who he is. Being in contradiction with himself, he creates conflict and thus is never at peace with himself. He escapes from reality in an endless struggle that only leads to antagonism, strife, bitterness, and sorrow. He spends his time wanting and then not wanting, remembering something, and then trying to forget it, pursuing one desire after another to seek gratification, with all his thinking being based on what happened in the past. He only feels alive because the constant struggle of contradiction provides him with a certain sense of vitality. But all that happens is that he pursues an intended result, trying to achieve an end through any means, which only leads to further contradiction. He operates by altering facts, he pursues authority, which only produces fear, and he resorts to his obstructive pattern of thought to deal with every challenge that arises. He functions as a repetitive machine in all political, economic, and social matters.

Trump's Actions

Trump is afraid of losing the respect of his family, of damaging his reputation among his followers, of being discovered as to who he really is, and most of all—of losing his wealth. In all that he possesses, he is afraid of anyone who disturbs them or who threatens to take them away. He is afraid of "losing" because that would cause him great pain. He shields himself psychologically because it would alter his sense of security if someone were to penetrate his psyche in a deep manner. He identifies himself with his party through a murky ideology in an attempt to restore the past and to prevent any significant change that will disturb his mental image of what he thinks things should be like. Thus, he will block any understanding of significant social activities because he does not want to be exposed to the stark realities of life. He may mouth the words that appear at face value to paint him as being very knowledgeable, but his actions only serve to undermine any of his expressions that he makes or actions that he takes.

Trump's life is consumed by old habits, customs, ideas, traditions, and memories. He becomes irritated whenever there is a situation where he is at odds with others, or where there is dissension in the ranks. His ambition suppresses others—even when very good advice is given to him. He makes choices in an impulsive manner without much thought given to any negative effects that may result from this. He makes ill-informed decisions, which may affect millions of people. His responses to challenges are always derived from his conditioning, and they are rooted in the past. He thinks that old solutions are the answer to new problems. He does not seem to think in practical ways, but mostly examines things in a very superficial manner.

Trump is caught up in the repetition of his own words—which are mainly lies—and which deny the truth, which he deems as being "fake news". For if he really thought that his words were the answer to all problems, then he would be a very happy man instead of the sullen, dour, angry, discontented, and ill-willed old man that he has become. Thus, he will never realize the truth because his actions all stem from lies, deceit, corruption, and mischief. And he will never change because he is incessantly involved in engaging in mindless trivialities and silly pettiness.

Trump Lives in Isolation

Trump has no capacity for warmth, affection, closeness, and togetherness with people, nor does he have any deep understanding of things and ideas. His quick responses to everything that occurs lacks an understanding that shows a true relationship. He distorts actuality by spouting off on what he would rather see happen instead of dealing with what is, and which therefore causes conflict. Most of his speeches are an escape into the future, which is merely a process of isolating himself from the present. And he only does things when there is some sort of gratification or adulation that is involved. Thus, he avoids facts and chooses to live in oblivion as he builds resistance to everything around him. In this manner he feels secure despite all of the disruptions that occur in his life.

Trump chooses to remain isolated, he promotes nationalism, and he clings to his conditioned responses through which he thinks he can create unity and peace. However, building barriers through isolation makes that goal an impossibility. It only serves to increase his power and to further separate society by means of a bureaucratic regime. He is solely interested in creating a society that is totally based on economics, industry, and the military. Yet, as he continues along this path, he creates further isolation, cloaking it behind his alleged patriotic spirit, and building even more resistance and conflict. He remains empty, dull, and weak even as he seeks to identify himself with something greater—be it race, religion, the party, the country, or God—in his desire for power. He has no real motive other than to create order by slick, clever and cunning means.

His Insincerity

Trump uses self-deception because it gives him a certain vitality. He utilizes this energy to impose his deceptions on others. His goal is to politically attain position, prestige, and power. It is an intent that is based on pure materialism rather than on necessity. In creating this deception, he becomes a slave to it, using it over and over again lest he run the risk of losing his followers and support. He pits one political party against the other, he pits the Muslim beliefs against the Christian beliefs, he pits whites against people of color, and he pits groups and organizations against each other.

Trump has never examined his life in a meaningful way and is mostly trapped in his own mental construct of who he is. He lives under a false identity that he has created for himself. He is intent on proving everyone else wrong, and he clearly does not seem to know what he wants to live for from an introspective view. He trusts no one, he tells lies about everything, he confuses what has transpired, and he often sees himself as a victim. He only identifies himself with his giant ego. He has no sincerity and so he creates boundaries, seeing life as a series of rivalries in which he must prevail.

Yet, this self-deception does not bring him any happiness or satisfaction for he falls deeper and deeper into a trap of his own making. He uses persuasion in every form to make people believe that he is sincere, but all the while he has sown the seeds of self-deception in a totally self-centered activity that has resulted in alienation. All his attempts to control, modify, interpret, or condemn social and political activities have become detrimental and destructive to everyone. In the end, he only manages to create chaos.

He Does Not Listen

Trump only pays attention to thoughts that confirm what he is saying. He does not listen to advice, pays no heed to criticisms, confines his attention span to very narrow exchanges, and certainly does not listen to discern the truth about matters. He is only interested in ceremonies that aggrandize his stature because he wants to have the approval of crowds. He initiates discontent and creates disharmony with his speeches at his rallies. He only wants agreement on everything that he says or does, and is not interested in cooperation, dialogue, or meaningful discussions.

Trump answers questions, but his responses are mostly superficial or else are attacks on the persons asking the questions. He seeks to downplay any differences of opinions and does not display clear thinking because his responses are meant to obfuscate things. In a very stubborn manner, he will not listen to any opposition or voices of reason. And since he depends on flattery, he probably wants to be the most famous person on earth to give him a sense of being remembered into immortality.

His Unmitigated Ambition

Trump's ambition seems to be one of creating a perfect system of order by means of exploitation and regimentation. Despite his power and wealth, he labors in a state of perpetual conflict. He competes with everyone, always seeking more money, greater prestige, a higher position, and attaining further influence while all the while perpetuating more conflict. His drive of personal ambition is certainly not based on his relationship with others. Rather, it comes from a lifelong desire to manipulate, to control, to acquire and to cajole others. He has an unrealistic dream of creating something wonderful for the country, but it is mired by useless projects such as building a border wall. His ambition only moves in a manner that induces more misery because he cannot buy love to create his perfect society. His compulsive behavior only results in more contradictions, which merely add to his destructive ambition that will only bring more hatred and strife.

Trump and Service

Although Trump states that he will fight to protect his country, it is mere propaganda. He did not serve his country when he was young by avoiding service through a feigned injury. He was never very active in politics throughout most of his life because he was too busy making money. He has never been involved in any social activities that promote benevolence or charity. And his sole economic motive has been to enrich himself at the expense of others. When he viewed the French gravesite of American soldiers who died in WWII, he asked General John Kelly "What was in it for them?"

Trump has played up to people, making a life of "winning" by being involved in questionable business practices, acting with deceit to always come out on top, to be right regardless of the facts, and to be of service to no one except himself. He only wants blind allegiance, acceptance of his authority, and respect for his material accomplishments— which have mostly been concentrated on the acquisition of property. He is not one whose aim is to be of service to those who are less fortunate.

His Thinking is Not Well-Organized

Trump's thinking reflects a sense of being used to getting his way all the time. His beginnings as a "spoiled brat" have only served to augment that type of thinking into his adult life. Although outwardly he dresses very orderly and maintains his immediate environment in immaculate condition, his inner thinking reflects a continuing disturbance that stems from his early years of rebellion. He is inconsiderate of others, he creates chaos to thrust himself into the limelight, and is always seeking attention—be it positive or negative.

Trump is not interested in reform because he has no deep feelings about anything. He tries to be intellectual, but his thinking reflects only a superficial sense of cleverness. He has no passion—other than anger—and his actions denote a very stubborn mind. He gets angry because he does not want to be hurt since that is his inner need for survival. Thus, he hurts others in return to take it out on everyone else in his aim of keeping his anger going. He protects himself by not being open, cooperative, or receptive, thus promulgating his nature of complete detachment. After all, in everything that he has done, it is apparent that he only wants to live in luxury and comfort, and in isolation so that nothing will affect him in the long run.

Trump and Beauty

Trump has eyes for outward beauty, which is reflected in his taste for clothes, in his gushing admiration for whom he views as beautiful women, in his relentless drive of constructing attractive buildings, and in his penchant for having nice furniture, jewelry, paintings and other accoutrements. However, his overly sensual attraction to the beauty of women has caused considerable disintegration in his life. Besides being accused by several women of unwanted encounters of sexual inappropriateness, he has bragged about being able to do anything that he wants to with women—simply because he is "a star". And women who have caused him problems have always been on the receiving end of his wrath, and thus they are no longer considered as beautiful to him. He treats women simply as objectified creatures of pleasure, with no real love involved and with no attachments.

He Does Not Favor Equality

Trump operates in a realm where he favors the haves over the have-nots. He has always surrounded himself with rich people, and he avoids mingling with the working masses—except as they are useful to him as props at his political rallies. Thus, he does not treat all people alike. Because he has a position of power as a CEO of his company, he feels entitled to run things as he wishes. He holds the power to give jobs—as well as to take them away—and he uses his position as leverage over everything. He craves status by meeting with ministers, governors, leaders of countries and ambassadors, all for the reason of enhancing his stature. Working class people are of no consequence to him except as voters and supporters. He also undermines minorities.

His Blueprint for America

Trump is intent on preparing for war while stating that he seeks peace. He probably thinks that his destiny is making the country into the greatest superpower that has ever existed. His probable goal is to create a culture in which conformity prevails and one in which everyone moves to a predetermined end of his choosing. His blueprint for the country consists of curtailing freedom: to control what women can do to their bodies, to restrict freedom of expression with very strong libel laws, to promote decisions that hinder the progress of minority groups, and to engender a form of police state that is ruled by weapons rather than the law. He is creating divisiveness, mistrust, hate and prejudice—all of which lead to aggression and despotism—and which will diminish the quality of life rather than embrace a culture that nurtures the human spirit.

Trump and the Sanctity of Life

Trump harps on abortion as if it was the greatest evil to ever beset mankind. However, he has no qualms about sending refugees who are seeking asylum back to their countries of origin where they will most likely be murdered. He has no problem with people on death row who will be executed. He has no hesitation about sending young men and women into war zones where they can be killed. He has no sympathy for those who are disadvantaged. He talks about peace but is intent on building more nuclear weapons. He negates global warming even though climate change will eventually kill thousands as a result of temperature extremes. He lauds dictators who indiscriminately butcher their own people. He pushes the Second Amendment as if it were a sacred law, yet tacitly condones the killing of innocents by military style weapons by refusing to support any gun restrictions. He is intent on building a wall to prevent dealers from crossing illegal drugs into the country but does nothing to stem the spread of opioids within the country, which are responsible for killing thousands.

Trump promotes coal mining in spite of the fact that the mineral has been responsible for thousands of deaths by people involved in its extraction. The burning of coal also creates more CO_2, thus elevating the already very high concentrations in the atmosphere that will push the earth towards a hothouse environment, which potentially will kill millions of species—as well as humans. He has removed many of the regulations concerning safety, thus endangering thousands who work in hazardous places. He has done away with environmental restrictions, thus putting millions at risk as a result of air, land, and water pollution. He has moved away from supporting alternative sources of energy such as wind, geothermal and solar power, which benefit the earth and reduce the sole reliance on fossil fuels that add to the existing CO_2 levels through combustion, and which could thereby save lives that would otherwise be affected by pollution.

Trump fundamentally does not care about the welfare and lives of people. Someone who pardons war criminals obviously has no feelings about the loss of innocent lives. Certainly, threatening countries with genocide shows that he has no regard for human life.

His Hypocrisy

Trump's double-talk has no limits and is without any virtue or morality. He accused his predecessor of playing golf instead of attending to his duties, yet he himself played golf for nearly one-fourth of the time that he was in office. He ranted about the Electoral College being unfair in a democracy until he won the 2016 election because of it, which he then labeled as a "genius" construct. Yet, when he lost the 2020 election by the same amount, he claimed that it was because of voter fraud that produced the difference in key states.

Trump claims to promote clean air and water yet is pushing "clean coal" and gutting the Environmental Protection Agency. He railed against the use of presidential executive orders as usurping the legislative power, but he has used this approach almost exclusively to promote his agendas. He paints others as liars, yet he makes stuff up on a whim. He criticized the use of private devices for government business, but he used an unsecure tweeter account as well as an unsecured mobile phone for all sorts of communication. He labeled the use of taxpayer money to pay for vacations as absurd while he racked up millions of dollars on his visits to his clubs—as well as making money off the rentals for everything that is involved for his personal security.

Trump frequently goes on tirades of complaining of reporters who use anonymous sources, while at the same time spouting off unsubstantiated claims of his own creation. He uses evangelicals to support his authenticity, and then does actions which are antithetical to the set of Christian ethics. He dwells on having respect for the flag and national anthem while disrespecting entire classes of citizens. He said that he would protect the DREAMers, but he has done nothing to accomplish this. He wants to appear as a loving and devoted husband while at the same time having been focused on prurient interests. There just is no end to his hypocrisy and it will continue unabated.

His Immorality

Trump is a leader who acts with aggressive behavior, who seeks absolute power, who subconsciously gives rise to hate and cruelty, and who surreptitiously undermines justice, equality, and freedom by means of unbridled authority. In his known sexual life, he has behaved without any regard to established norms. In his business dealings, he has refused several times to pay contractors for their work, he has overcharged customers in his rental properties, he has promoted schemes to obtain money by offering nothing in return, such as Trump University, he has declared bankruptcy seven different times to get out of debt, and he has dealt with banks in sometimes shady operations—all for the sake of making as much money as he can. He has written books that are all geared towards conning people. He even created a foundation, which never benefitted any charities. He considers migrants, refugees, and immigrants as less than desirable people and he shows contempt for minorities. These are not the characteristics of a moral person. Instead, this is someone who functions without ethics. The ease in which he dispenses with ethical behaviors makes it appear sometimes that he might have a tendency to be sociopathic—or in the extreme, even psychopathic.

He is Vindictive

Trump is viciously vindictive. He is vindictive toward his enemies, a group that includes Speaker Nancy Pelosi, Representatives Adam Schiff and Liz Cheney, former FBI Director James Comey and Senators Mitt Romney, Mitch McConnell and Mike Rounds. He behaves with malice and with a total lack of charity such as he did with NBA teams and the Women's Olympic soccer team who refused to come to the White House.

In 1999, when Trump's father died, he cut his deceased brother's family out of the will. Not only that but he withdrew the medical benefits that were critical to his nephew's infant child. He chose to make cheating on his first wife front-page news. He chose to advertise the sexual superiority of his new mistress over the mother of his children.

When those close to him fell out of favor, he unceremoniously expelled them from the White House. He badmouthed Dr. Tony Fauci over the coronavirus pandemic—a disdain for science and expertise. He went after Joe Biden with fury and lies, calling him senile. He doubted that Kamala Harris was a United States citizen, just like he previously had done with President Barack Obama.

His vindictiveness renders him incapable of taking the high road. He is a graduate of the University of Pennsylvania where he threatened legal action if his grades ever were disclosed. The desire to matter and feel significant among his supporters is associated with his support for hostile and vindictive actions against his political rivals. He uses his supporters to contest the system and to engage in aggressive actions directed against the government. After he was acquitted from the first impeachment, he launched a vindictive tirade as he furiously meandered through a list of grievances. And, when Vice President Mike Pence refused to comply with his wishes of rejecting the Electoral College votes, he dissed him as not having a backbone—even tweeting it to his supporters who then wanted to hang Pence with some gallows.

There is no respite from his vindictiveness as he will always continue to engage in his retribution harangues.

The Whining Big Baby

Trump is a big baby who picks on people that threaten his authority. He keeps whining about losing the 2020 election, insisting that it was stolen from him. He also keeps saying that the election is far from over, ignoring the official tally that shows that he lost. He can't even demonstrate the behavior of an adolescent because he has refused to abide by any rules. He continues to act like the biggest baby that has ever been seen, so much so that the British created an inflatable balloon as a caricature of Trump, depicting him as an angry orange baby holding a smartphone, with a snarling mouth, tiny hands, and wearing a diaper. The balloon was flown in Parliament Square when Trump visited London in 2018.

Trump has the reactive profile of a small child. He seethes like an irritable four-year-old instead of exhibiting any kind of restraint. He whined about receiving bad publicity when in his mind he was doing an excellent job as President. He is an emotional equivalent of a toddler. He can't articulate the rage that he feels, and the questions at his news conferences only made him angrier. Thus, he got extra attention whenever he threw a temper tantrum—just like a child. And when equal anger is directed at him, he resorts to name-calling, escalating the situation in his emotionally stunted manner. His blustering is beyond anger management techniques because all that he yearns for is praise. When he doesn't get this, he embarks on a tirade of publicly bullying others in a hurtful way.

Trump always has to be the center of attention. He will say outrageous things and make crazy proclamations. He will constantly brag about how great he is. What matters the most to him is that he must always have the focus on him because that is what is important to him, despite his lies, denials, and irresponsibility. Thus, he blames others for picking on him and that becomes his justification for his behavior, which is usually revenge—something that is attributable to a pre-school child.

The Proverbial Clown

Trump became a clown with his political circus that he engendered. He encouraged people to be as uninhibited in their stupidity as he is. But real clowns are virtuosos whereas Trump is not. There is an artistry that goes into being a clown—which Trump totally lacks. Yet in his own way Trump is a clown. T-shirts were sold with the following message printed on them: "Elect a clown, expect a circus". This was a very astute observation of the events at the White House during his tenure.

His association with Rudy Giuliani as his lawyer produced some hilarious moments, including the press conference at the Four Seasons Landscaping Company where Giuliani engaged in a clown shouting fraud. He hung around with the "My Pillow" guy, Michael Lindell, who claimed he had an enormous database with proof that Trump won the election.

Trump's antics at his rallies are like that of a ringmaster entertaining his audience. His press conferences were antagonistic with him acting like a buffoon. His television appearances were those of a showman, always looking to punctuate the moment with a clever witticism. And his presidential addresses were like performances emulating someone on a high wire act. But they were not funny because all the while "the house was burning" and all that he could do was twiddle his thumbs—acting much like Nero watching Rome burn while he played his fiddle.

Trump's Personality

Trump represents an enigma regarding his personality. He is a very complex person who creates his own reality—even when the facts do not support it. His identity was shaped by his past by how he assessed the human condition from his position of wealth and status. He has made every effort to prove the correctness of his position—even after the fact. His identity in life is that of a person who does not contribute to the quality of other people's lives. Instead, it is focused on a habitual and narcissistic view of himself. It is all about image, even if stems from self-deception and illusion, in order to present himself in the most favorable light.

He was outrageous, pompous, spiteful, vindictive, and mean-spirited in his numerous rallies and press conferences. He was driven to damage others and to pursuing his grandiose dreams—even though he was psychologically damaged. His pathology of indifference, idiocy, lunacy, delusion, and violence manifested in his desire for adulation. His mediocrity was displayed by his bullying, blustering and cruelty, despite his labeling himself as "a stable genius". His rage, impulsiveness, hubris, ruthlessness, sometimes clownish antics, and discontent showed that he was unfit for the office.

Trump is most likely not an evil person per se, and he cares for his family—even though they probably do not meet his expectations of them. He possesses an enigmatic, complex, and egocentric personality that defies psychological explanations. He hardly ever smiles, he almost never laughs, and most of the time he is either frowning or expressing anger. He lies at every turn, he makes up stuff, and he denies everything.

Trump is certainly one hundred percent ego because in his world everything revolves around him, and leaves no room for compassion, benevolence, kindness, or love. Since he functions without integrity or responsibility, his actions are done solely to benefit his goals and to further his influence among his supporters. In many ways he is like a pied piper who entrances the crowds at his rallies with his nonsense rhetoric.

By growing up in New York City, Trump was exposed to an environment filled with bustling activity—but also in a city that is chaotic and replete with conflict, strife, and confusion. But he was not only shaped by his environment. Growing up in a wealthy family also influenced his views. As a privileged offspring, he viewed his stature as being above everyone else. His father also had a huge impact during his formative years while his mother appears to have been an enabler. Also, when he got into the real estate business with his dad, he met a very clever and cunning lawyer, Roy Cohn, who became his mentor, and who taught him how to lie, deceive, counterpunch, obfuscate, distract and deny—as well as to litigate everything.

Trump is an old man now and he will not change his ways. He will never experience anything else except what he values most, which is money. It is unknown what his purpose in life is since he has never shared that with anyone. He reacts to any criticism in a negative way, sometimes even being vicious by disparaging the person who chose to malign him, made fun of him or who has countered his views. He expects everyone to obey him, to follow his plan of action, and to support him in every way possible. Above all, he wants loyalty from people around him—even though he is not loyal himself to anyone other than maybe his oldest daughter, Ivanka. He trusts no one, he is afraid of being found out, and he operates as a slick con man.

Trump is the epitome of a totally self-absorbed person, and a master of deceit. He can be outrageous with his commentaries, he has little regard for the law, he uses threats in attempts to make people comply with his agenda, and he has disdain for minorities whom he views as being inferior. He brags about himself, he touts his intellect as that of having superior knowledge, he disparages the intelligence of those who attack him, and he never apologizes for his behavior—no matter what he does or says. He exploits people, using them to his advantage, praising them temporarily, and then dumping them when they are no longer useful to him. He does and says whatever he wants to without any regard to the consequences. This is the essence of who Trump is—a very unenlightened human being—who will be 78 years old in 2024 if he runs for President.

What Trump's Handwriting Reveals

In 1988, the world-renowned graphologist and court-recognized document examiner, Felix Klein, did a handwriting analysis of Donald Trump without knowing who it was. With only his gender and age but without his signature, which might identify him, Klein analyzed the handwriting. Afterwards, the name was revealed to him, and he completed his analysis by viewing the signature. This is what he found:

Aside from Trump's overly large, narcissistic signature, Klein found that his writing revealed the immense insecurity, aggressiveness, and rigid inability to think and perceive the world accurately. He said that Trump was grandiose, extremely narcissistic, and paranoid—so much so that he considered him delusional. Moreover, he noted that Trump was unable to relate to other humans with any degree of emotional attachment or consideration. People to him were objects, only useful to feed his insatiable need for adoration and attention.

In looking specifically at his signature, Klein explained that Trump's rigidly angular letter connections formed what he called shark's teeth, which is indicative of rage and the capacity for being extremely aggressive, acting out behaviors. He continued by saying that Trump was a very dangerous individual, capable of all manner of criminal behavior and that he was a menace to society. He went on to say that Trump was hypo-manic and determined to get whatever he wanted, describing him as a "screaming locomotive running down the tracks without any brakes". He added that God help anyone who tries to stop him. He finished with these words: "I have probably examined well over 200,000 handwriting samples over more than 60 years, and Trump's writing is one of the worst that I have ever seen. In fact, the only writing that comes to mind that is as bad is Charles Manson's".

His Tarnished Legacy

While some portion of his appeal was based on legitimate grievances of working-class people against elites, Trump instead awakened an authoritarian impulse among the citizenry that was larger and more rabid—as well as more easily triggered. Even so, his actions did not do very much to help his minions. The oath of office that he swore to did not mean anything to him since he did not care about anything or anyone else except himself. And he displayed a total lack of remorse for everything that happened as well as anything that he said.

Despite having made a promise to deal with the crumbling infrastructure in the United States, President Trump did nothing in his four years in office to start any projects to rebuild America—other than his medieval border fence. Instead, he spent most of his time watching television, tweeting, and golfing at every opportunity that he could. He also disbanded the infrastructure advisory board. His former Secretary of State, Rex Tillerson, called him a "fucking moron" who was dumb and lazy and who had trouble understanding more than two issues at a time.

Before Trump, James Buchanan was the worst President in American history for his failure to avert a Civil War. In contrast, Trump tried to initiate a civil war by dividing the country with his rhetoric. He acted like a mob boss, with little or no regard for the country's institutions. He was even impeached, becoming the third President charged by the House, and only a Republican-led Senate acquitted him on the charges of obstruction of Congress and abuse of power. Then, he was impeached again for inciting an insurrection, becoming the only President to be impeached twice. Since there was not enough time to conduct a trial before the end of his term, the trial was postponed until later under the Biden administration where he was acquitted again. In the end, it all came crashing down on him because he could never tell the truth and because he could never accept the fact that he lost, thus becoming the thing that he hated the most: that of being a loser.

Trump had no government experience nor any in-depth knowledge of the functioning of the three branches of government. The worst part was his incompetence in dealing with the coronavirus pandemic. From his early conversation with President Xi of China, he knew that the coronavirus was very deadly, but he did not prepare for it. Consequently, the death toll ended at 404,000 deaths on his last day as President with over 24 million Americans being infected. For this alone, he will be regarded as a tyrant, buffoon, clown, and incompetent chief executive as well as being a delusional, deranged, sociopath and psychopath. At no point during his four years in office did Trump act presidential other than to nominate three Supreme Court Justices.

Trump will probably be regarded as the worst President in United States history and the only one to have been impeached twice. His presidency ended in discord, division, and disgrace that encapsulates the pandemonium of his single term—one which was marked by vindictiveness and neglect. It culminated in him inciting an insurrection against Congress—one that will leave a legacy of chaos, contempt and a hateful political environment that will take years to purge from the American psyche. As such, it will be the most despicable act that will forever be a huge part of his legacy: his coordinated and orchestrated attack of the Capitol building by a violent mob of his fervent followers in which 8 people died—and his unwillingness to stop it or to condemn the rioters.

Conclusion

Donald Trump has functioned all his life by manipulating everything and everyone. He has made the acquisition of wealth as the shining example of his success—even though he has been beset by bankruptcies, lawsuits, failed businesses and questionable enterprises. He has disparaged everyone who has said anything against him, made fun of him or criticized him. He uses crass and crude expressions to show his disdain for others. He constantly brags about himself in which he views himself as being superior to everyone else.

Although he has created vast holdings in real estate, his methods of achieving them are suspect since they are unknown because he conceals his financial transactions. He does not pursue any path that leads to enlightenment—for himself or others—and he acts with compulsiveness in every encounter rather than taking time to think about what he says or does. Trump is devoid of any spirituality, and his whole agenda is one of winning—at any cost. Thus, he has no conscience about his behaviors and how they affect others.

Trump has little self-awareness, is not introspective, does not meditate on things, and shows no interest in becoming a better person. He is someone with a very huge ego who craves adulation, demands loyalty—even though he has none—who constantly lies to distract from his mischievous doings, and who depicts himself as the savior of the world. He may not be evil, but he is certainly not a good person. In its bad aspects, Trump represents the unpolished side of human nature. If you listen to what he says with complete attention, and if you notice what he does with total observation, you will perceive who he is: an unenlightened human being who only imparts prejudice, falsehoods, hate, and confusion.

Bibliography

Abramson, Seth. *Proof of Collusion: How Trump Betrayed America*. New York City: Simon & Schuster, 2018.

Cohen, Michael. *Disloyal: A Memoir: The True Story of the Former Personal Attorney to President Donald J. Trump*. New York City: Skyhorse, 2020.

D'Antonio, Michael. *The Truth About Trump*. New York City: St. Martin's Griffin, 2016.

Fraser, John L. *The Truth Behind Trump Derangement Syndrome: "There is more than meets the eye'*. Hong Kong: JF Publications, 2018.

Johnston, David Cay. *It's Worse Than You Think: What the Trump Administration is Doing to America*. New York City: Simon & Schuster, 2018.

Kranish, Michael and Marc Fisher. *Trump Revealed: An American Journey of Ambition, Ego, Money, and Power*. New York City: Scribner, 2016.

Lee, Bandy. *The Dangerous Case of Donald Trump*. New York City: Martin's Press, 2017.

Miller, Greg. *The Apprentice: Trump, Russia, and the Subversion of American Democracy*. New York City: Custom House, 2018.

Trump. Mary L. *Too Much and Never Enough: How My Family Create the World's Most Dangerous Man*. New York City: Simon & Schuster, 2020.

Wilson, Rick. *Everything Trump Touches Dies: A Republican Strategist Gets Real About the Worst President Ever*. New York City: Free Press, 2018.

Wolff, Michael. *Fire and Fury: Inside the Trump White House*. New York City: Henry Holt and Co., 2018. New York City: Gallery Books, 2020.

_____. *Siege: Trump Under Fire*. New York City: Henry Holt and Co., 2019.

Woodward, Bob. *Fear: Trump in the White House*. New York City: Simon & Schuster, 2018.

_____. *Rage:* New York City: Simon & Schuster, 2020.

Zirin, James D. *Plaintiff in Chief: A Portrait of Donald Trump in 3,500 Lawsuits*. New York City: All Points Books, 2019.